Job Screener for Locum Tenens Jobs

By: Lorraine Barron, MD

Locums Lifestyle
1923 Bragg St #140-2543
Sanford, NC 27330
www.LocumsLifestyle.org

Copyright © 2013 by Lorraine Barron, MD
All rights reserved. No part of this book may be copied, transmitted or stored in a database without permission.

DISCLAIMER

This book is not intended as medical advice. It is also not intended to prevent, diagnose, treat or cure disease. Instead the book is intended only to share the unofficial research and opinion of the author. The information is provided for educational purposes only, not as treatment instructions for any disease or ailment. Much of the book is a statement of opinion in areas where the facts are controversial or do not exist. The information in this book should not be considered any more valid than any other type of informal opinion.

The information was not written to replace the advice or care of a qualified health care professional. Be sure to check with your own qualified health care provider before beginning any protocols or procedures discussed in this book, or before stopping or altering any diet, lifestyle, or other therapies previously recommended to you by your health care provider.

The treatments described in this book may have side effects and carry other known and unknown risks and health hazards. The statements in this book have not been evaluated by the United States FDA. Use of the information in this book is at your own risk.

This book is dedicated to Carl and Olivia.
Who remind me daily that I can't take money or work with
me when I die.

A Message to All Locum Tenens

Welcome to Locums Lifestyle, thank you for your interest in the job screener. Be sure to check your email for updates from Dr. Barron (drbarron@locumslifestyle.org).

Once we receive the form we will enter your hospital review into our extensive database. This is an anonymous process, when we receive it other hospitalists and doctors (including you) are able to look at other hospitals and decide before you even consider interviewing there if it's a place you'd like to work. Knowing the pertinent information about each hospital will allow you to guide your initial interview with them and know exactly what to expect.

This form is also useful because you can save it and fill it out for yourself every time you consider an interview with a new hospital. It is perfect for record keeping and making sure you don't get lost in the details. Writing everything down and saving it creates better organization which creates a better locums doctor. Included in your download is a report explaining each question and why it's important to be asking those questions. So if you're new to locums or you've had experience you'll understand why each section is important.

For more inquiries on the Job Screener, feel free to send me an email.

All the best,
Lorraine Barron, MD
drbarron@locumslifestyle.org

TABLE OF CONTENTS

A Message to All Locum Tenens 5
Hospitalist Questionnaire 7
Questionnaire Breakdown 9
    Facility 9
    Locum Company 9
        1. Name and Number of the Hospital Contact 9
        2. How Many Doctors in the Group? 9
        3. PA/NP Supervision Required? 10
        4. Is There an Admitter Shift Available? 10
        5. Number and Type of Beds in the Hospital 11
        6. Average Number of Patients 11
        7. Average Number of Admissions 11
        8. Subspecialists 11
        9. ICU Availability 12
        10. Shift Time 12
        11. Handoff Protocol 12
        12. EMR Availability 13
        13. CPOE 13
        14. Progress Noted: Typed, Handwritten or Dictated 14
        15. Hospital Credentialing Time Frame 14
Recommended Reading 15
About The Author 26

HOSPITALIST QUESTIONNAIRE

Facility:

Locum Company:

Hospital Contact:

Date:

1. Name and Number of Head Hospitalist:

2. Number of Doctors:

3. PA/NP Supervision (circle one):

    Yes   No

4. Admitter Shift Available (circle one):

    Yes   No

5. Total Number of Beds:

    a. Number of Medicine Beds:

    b. Number of ICU Beds:

6. Average Census of Patients/Doc:

Lorraine Barron, MD

7. Average Number of Admissions/Doc:

8. Subspecialists Available:

   Pulmonary *Cardiology* *Critical Care:*
   Yes/No **Yes/No** *on call or on site*
   Yes/No

   Surgery *AMI management* *Psychiatry*
   Yes/No **Yes/No** **Yes/No**

   Stroke Center *Neurology* *Urology*
   Yes/No **Yes/No** **Yes/No**

9. ICU:

   Open   Closed

10. Shift length (circle one):

    6a-6p   7a-7p   7p-7a

    Swing shift
    Yes/No

11. Shift Hand off Protocol (circle one):

    Face-to-face   Telephone   Written

12. EMR:

13. CPOE

    Yes   No

14. Progress Notes (circle one):

    Written   Typed   Dictated

Questionnaire Breakdown

Facility

When you speak with so many hospitals, it's actually hard to keep them all-straight. Save this form to refresh your memory of you look at the facility later. Be sure to include if the position is with a management company.

Locum Company

Once you've gone to the facility you have to keep using the same locum companies at that facility if they have your CV. The deal between the hospital and the locum company usually has a "non compete" clause that keeps you from being presented by another company for two years. This is why you need to keep track of which locum company for each hospital. Be sure to date the form too.

1. Name and Number of the Hospital Contact

It's important to document who you're interviewing. If there is a discrepancy later about how the job was represented this will give you back up documentation. The preference would be the medical director of the group. However, there are some groups that are in flux and you can't get the medical director and you'll be speaking to an administrative person. Their level of knowledge about the group is usually different and it's usually a sign of a poorly organized group or possibly a controlling administration. Use this when looking a "deal breakers" and your acceptable rates.

2. How Many Doctors in the Group?

This number gives you a base to confirm the patient volume and admission match what you are being told. A three-person group with

10 admissions a day is busier than a ten-person group with 10 admissions a day.

3. PA/NP Supervision Required?

PA/NP will actually add quite a bit of work to the workload when you're locums, especially if you're not familiar with their quality. Some places can try to force you to supervise the PA's 12 patients in addition to your 18- a disaster waiting to happen. Additionally, you're not getting paid to see 30 patients, why take the liability for it? Few are safe doing this given the high level of acuity we generally see. Even when they are "good", physicians tend to overestimate their knowledge base. Additionally, the rules on supervision vary from state to state and you make not be able to supervise if you're not "assigned" through the medical board.

I make a rule of almost never supervising. Sometimes an exception can be made where the midlevel is in the ER- checks a patient directly out with you- and then you follow up on the patient on the same day when they arrive to the floor. But, that situation does not arise often. This allows you to get that question out early and decide if it's a "deal breaker". Most of the time, you can just tell them "I don't supervise due to liability reasons, I'll be happy to take on a couple of extra patients". So that allows you to set the stage upfront and not have an issue after arriving to the job. This is both a rate-changer and deal breaker question.

4. Is There an Admitter Shift Available?

Usually this is a shift where you only do admissions. You might work from 11AM till 7 PM just doing admissions and there are no (or little) rounding duties. Most of the time, you just sit on the ER and do admissions. This is actually a nice shift. If it's available it's very easy for locums to come in and get started really quickly making sure you're done quickly and be done on time.

5. Number and Type of Beds in the Hospital

This gives you an idea of the level of acuity that the hospital can handle and the degree that the hospitalist group runs the facility. If you're looking at a hundred-bed hospital with 2 ICU beds, most likely the hospital cannot manage critically ill patients and you're going to spend more of your time (and liability) transferring patients to a higher level of care. As opposed to having a 250-bed hospital that might have 10 ICU beds. It's also important to note, in general, if that's the only hospitalist group in the hospital in a 200-bed place and there's only 3 hospitalists rounding- that group is probably being overworked. That's not necessarily a deal breaker, but it might be a "rate changer."

6. Average Number of Patients

This is a "rate changer" number. The Society Hospital Medicine recommends the average 15 patients per doc with no more encounters than 18 a day to include the admissions. Everyone says they see 15-18, but a good chunk of them are actually more than that. If they're telling you that they're already seeing 20 patients per doc a day you can almost guarantee that it's even higher than that. So it's a good gauge to see what the hospital is trying to portray their volume as being.

7. Average Number of Admissions

This is a "truth in disclosure" number. If they tell you that they're rounding on 15 but there are 4-5 patients per doc a day, there is a good chance they are misrepresenting the correct volume. To keep the patient census at 15 with 5-day admissions would require 5 discharges a day and NO admissions overnight- not a likely scenario.

8. Subspecialists

This section will help you determine your rate and liability risk. It also helps you gage the level of acuity the hospital can handle. Transferring patients due to lack of specialists increases the work volume and liability. It should be considered when determining your acceptable rate. The same issue goes for neurology, cardiology (interventional or not), and nephrology. This also affects the acceptable census level.

9. ICU Availability

A closed ICU usually makes floor rounding quicker and a census average of 18- 20 manageable for a 12-hour shift.

That's a different situation then an open ICU with 20 beds and little pulmonary support. It can be a "rate changer" (or possibly a deal breaker) and be tempered by group size.

10. Shift Time

On average almost all shifts are 12 hours, occasional places you can see shorter than 12 but you have to remember you're getting paid less when that happens. So, it would need to be a nice facility where they're giving you a fairly paid for a shorter shift. This might be acceptable in a "resort" area where you want to spend part of your day doing something else (i.e. like the beach or skiing). Most places do 7p to 7anight shift.

Consider the average number of admission with this and factor in if you have a swing shift helping you out. Swing shifts are all at different times. If I see a facility that wants you to work 6a-6p you start to think they're probably being a little too rigid, because frankly most people don't want to come in at 6 o'clock in the morning. If that works for you, consider charging a higher rate- most people don't like getting up that early!

11. Handoff Protocol

This can really affect the length of your day (good and bad). Some groups require a face-to-face check out. So when you finish at the end of the day and your shift might end at 7 and the night guy shows up at 7, but it takes 30 min to check out your patients. Compare this to leaving them a note and going back to the hotel with your pager at 5pm. The downside is that you're "stuck" in the hospital. This upside- you have a higher chance of billing overtime at $200/hr. Groups with no check out procedures are usually not that well-organized and can be a higher liability risk if you're doing a night shift. This issue is usually a rate-changer.

12. EMR Availability

There are many of different brands and all a little bit different, but some are user-friendlier than others. Try to expose yourself to as many different systems as possible. Even the same system can be set up differently from place to place. It's a good "selling point" when you're negotiating your rate. The more experience you have, the more you'll find they all have the same pattern- like using a radio in different cars. If it's a new EMR system, charge a higher rate. It usually takes a hospital system 3-6 months to begin to regain efficiency and they staff is usually "extra stressed". I only accept that kind of job, if I'm the "extra" person making up for the lost productivity.

13. CPOE

Computer Physician Order Entry. Depending on the EMR it can make your life a lot easier or it can make it really bad. This is especially true if the order sets are not appropriately put in the computer. Lack of order sets or poorly organized order sets can make a frustrating day. It again revisits liability. If you're in a facility trying to put chest pain orders but there is no aspirin, stress test or nitroglycerine on the chest pain orders and you have to go back and re-order that in a separate section. It ups your risk of making errors if it's not a good EMR program. This can be both a rate changer or deal breaker and again this is something you have to consider when you're looking at a facility.

14. Progress Noted: Typed, Handwritten or Dictated

Everybody is different. Some people can get through written notes quicker, others typed or dictated. So this is just another factor in your overall decision.

15. Hospital Credentialing Time Frame

Credentialing time frame is to help you decide some on how badly the facility needs you. If they say they can turn it around in 2 weeks that means they must be pretty short and that they're hurrying trying to get somebody in. This can help you when negotiating your rates.

The higher the need, the higher the rate. If they're telling you it takes 60 days to get you credentialed, that tells you that it is a facility that is not well-organized, that's heavily bureaucratic and you may not want to bother with all the credentialing. You will spend unpaid time getting everything together. A lot of times they'll continue to ask for pieces of information they didn't originally want. Also remember that if you're not credentialed, your exhibit is null and void. This can be a problem if they wait until 2 days prior to the start date you're not credentialed. It can block the days that would have been open to another facility. The typical is 30-45 if they get it done in that time frame then that's usually not too painful.

Recommended Reading

During my research on freelance jobs, I found these to be helpful. You can check them out on my site here:

http://LocumsLifestyle.org/recommended

The Locum from her Past

A medical romance novel about two Locum doctors –Katie, a committed and overworked doctor working alone in her country practice and Tom, still bitter from a painful 11 year marriage and the man that broke Katie's heart 12 years ago

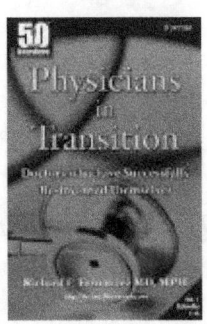

Physicians in Transition: 25 doctors who successfully reinvented themselves

This is a book about extraordinary individuals who have surpassed a lot of challenges to find their career satisfaction and personal happiness.

Principles and Practice of Hospital Medicine

This book aims to give trainees, junior and senior clinicians, and other professionals with a complete source that they can utilize to improve care processes and performance in the hospitals that serve their communities.

Essentials of Hospital Medicine: A Practical Guide for Clinicians

This is the single source needed for hospitalists striving to deliver outstanding care and provide value to their patients and hospitals.

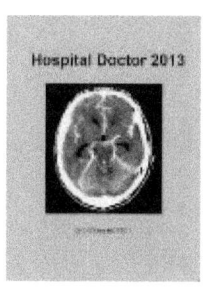

Hospital Doctor 2013

A book that tackles on management of acute medical and surgical emergencies as well as general ward management issues for new and experienced doctors. Its not just a text and list of instructions but contains pathophysiology and useful clinical pearls.

Do You Feel Like You Wasted All That Training

The combination of personal experience and doctor-to-doctor advice in this book is very entertaining and helps readers interested in non-clinical careers for physicians, navigate the five phases of their physician career change: introspection, exploration, preparation, acquisition, and transition.

The 4 Hour Work Week

If you are dreaming of escaping the rat race, travelling the word and earning a monthly five-figure income, The 4-Hour Workweek is the blueprint for just living more and working less.

Quitter

This book is based on 12 years of cubicle living and a true story of cultivating a dream job that changed the author's life and the world in the process.

Non-Clinical Careers for Physicians

Have a regular schedule to spend more time with your family. Recapture the career passion you once had. Get paid by what you are worth. This book will guide you to the new path that you aim for!

Never Lose Again

This book reveals a simple but remarkably effective set of fifty questions that anyone can immediately use to become far better negotiators.

A Physician's Comprehensive Guide to Negotiating

This book is dedicated to physicians to help them with their negotiating skills in order for them to get what they deserve with over 200 examples which tells them exactly the dos and don'ts of negotiation.

About The Author

Lorraine Barron, MD is the founder of LocumsLifestyle.org, a website dedicated to supporting freelance physicians and helping others transition to the freelance lifestyle. She has practiced medicine as a Hospitalist for the past 10 years and prior to that, was one of the first female physicians to take over as Medical Department Head for the Seabees while in the Navy. She currently works as a freelance physician in multiple states when she's not traveling (for fun) or spending time with family.

You can find Dr. Barron on Google+ and on Facebook. It is her goal to help other physicians gain control of their careers and realize their possibilities.

www.ingramcontent.com/pod-product-compliance
Lightning Source LLC
Chambersburg PA
CBHW070735180526
45167CB00004B/1760